God, Me, or Karma

God, Me, or Karma

TINA RED

Published by TR Wordsmith Publishing
Chicago, IL

GOD, ME, OR KARMA

This is a work of non-fiction. All poems in this
book are original works of the author. Any
similarities to other works are coincidental.

ISBN-13: 978-0-578-63903-1

Published by TR Wordsmith Publishing
Chicago, IL

Printed in the United States of America
First Edition February 2020

Design: Make Your Mark Publishing Solutions
Editing: Make Your Mark Publishing Solutions

Contents

ACKNOWLEDGEMENTS

"She believed she could, so she did."

I have to start by thanking God for giving me this talent and strength. My Father for seeing my gift with words early on and cultivating it. My mom and my family (Talithia, Amanda, Anastasia, Carl, Donald, Patrick and Allegra) for always being there for me.

My best friend, Brandi; her belief and pushiness were the origins of The Wordsmith. My English teacher, Ms. Milsap, turned friend, Teri. She sealed the deal that the art of English and writing would be my life's work. My bestie/sister circle—Montia, Candice, Sharita, and boo thangs, Nikki, Nikki, Jessica, Kimberly, and Arlene, for being the biggest group of supporters a girl could ask for. Enitan Bereola II for giving me the final push into my destiny. Davida for helping me embark on the road that led me here. My EGL sisters, Novia, Ericka, and Kisha, for helping me find my voice again.

To all the ones I didn't name—thank you! I have a *huge* support system and not enough money to list you all because this costs by the word. Tuh!

To all my new boo thangs, a.k.a. book readers, I appreciate you! There were so many other books to choose from and so many other things to spend your coins on. I thank you for choosing to read my—well, *our*—journey, and I hope you enjoy.

Tina Red - The Wordsmith

Contributors

More than a Personal Self-Publishing Assistant, Monique Mensah, owner of Make Your Mark Publishing Solutions, brought *God, Me, or Karma* to life with her expertise and dream team designers. The reason you're physically holding this book (or scrolling through the eBook) is because of her. From editing, to the book cover, to print, she handled it all.

Monique, I can't thank you enough! If you're an aspiring writer, my gift to you is her contact information below:

Monique D. Mensah

Make Your Mark Publishing Solutions

Web: www.makeyourmarkps.com

Email: info@makeyourmarkps.com

DEDICATION

I dedicate this book to all those who suffer in silence.

Always remember, it's not just you and you're not alone.

Introduction

It was either my pen or the pen—feel me?

LOVE.

A four-letter word that holds much power. Too much power if you ask me.

See, LOVE has never been as good to me as I was to it. Between you and me, I don't even know if I've ever experienced real love. Maybe it was just real lust, real infatuation, and real delusions of grandeur that tainted my perception of what I've heard is a beautiful thing. Regardless, for me, LOVE was ugly. And hurt. To the core.

Amid all the turmoil LOVE brought my way, I never once cried out in anguish, nor did I ask for help. Instead, I learned an unhealthy coping skill of suffering in silence and lived under the black woman creed of "Fuck it; I'll do it myself." I used Hennessey to numb the pain coupled with partying and any other vices to keep from going insane.

A lot of you reading this know exactly what I'm talking about because you, too, have done the same. Some of you still are. And that's a dark, dangerous, and lonely place. So this book—this book is for you.

Why a poetry and prose book?

The pages of this book are how I broke the unhealthy habit of suffering in silence and began the road to healing.

These works were never supposed to see the light of day. I was struggling through trauma and toxic memories as I wrote my first novel (coming 2020) when it was laid on my heart to compile and release the pages you are preparing to read. I fought against it for a long time because this wasn't my plan—I wanted to be a novelist, not a poet. And I certainly didn't want to air out the lowest, most vulnerable parts of my life to the world. The thought alone induced anxiety. We were all curating our lives for the world before social media existed, even though most of us never realized it. My assembled persona was strong, invincible, and neatly held together in the face of all adversity like a straight-up G. How could I go against what I'd spent years building? And at the high personal cost I'd paid?

I now understand it's not about me, my wants or fears, and it has never been. I realize my suffering was never in vain. Instead, it was preparing me for this very moment and the road I didn't quite know I'd be traveling.

Poetry and prose were the outlets that allowed me to release the hurt and anger and finally start healing.

For years, I screamed, cried, and hemorrhaged on these pages while suffering in silence behind what I thought was love—unknowingly for you. I suffered alone so you no longer have to.

My healing, my way.

I'm healing to be a voice for all those who think it's only them. Trust me when I say *it's not*. But you don't have to explain anything to me. I understand how you feel on an entire spiritual level. Been there, done that a good fifty-'leven times. I even tattooed it on my body hoping the physical pain would help the internal anguish subside (it didn't), so I'd know it was real (it wasn't).

This isn't just my story—it's all of our stories. It's also not solely a "woman's tale" because there's no gender bias for selfish people. I know men hurt and need to heal, too. Men, unfortunately, suffer in silence more than women based on the way society dictates their masculinity. For all my male readers, this is a safe zone. You, too, can relate without feeling judged or bashed. My heart aches at the knowledge that many of you will never know what it feels like to freely express yourself the way I have throughout this book. Rest assured, I never lost sight of that and kept you in mind as I created *our* story.

Just know, I broke through my silence and pride for the person who loves hard but never gets it back in return.

For the person who internalizes their pain because they're supposed to be the pillar of strength for everyone.

For the person who feels destined to build people up only for them to try to destroy you.

For the person who fixes all those around them yet feels broken.

For the protector of many who sometimes feels regarded by none.

For the person who's mad as hell (with every right to be) but villainized for holding resentment for having their time wasted and being deceived.

I took my pen and penned all those pent-up emotions that keep you awake at night as you continuously replay the failed scenarios. Those feelings that keep you scared of love and from fully giving yourself.

I wrote through the pain, prosed through the anger, and free versed my way into healing and forgiveness to show that feelings of hurt, hate, self-loathing, weakness, and despair are fleeting and can be replaced with love, acceptance, strength, and forgiveness. Healing isn't a straight road. You will make pitstops at Anger Ave., Resentment Rd., Backslide Blvd., and Depression St., but you will eventually find your way to the light on the other side of your darkest moments.

Don't get me wrong, I'm not fully healed, but I've come a long way. At times, this kumbaya, Iyanla Vanzant type shit can and does turn into some "redrum," split-their-wig type shit, but focusing on my own healing and growth circumvents any ill will. By the same token, while I refuse to let them steal anymore of my future, I wish *I would* stay silent about our pasts.

You shouldn't either. It's time to stop suffering in silence.

If they didn't want our grievances aired in public, they shouldn't have been comfortable hurting us in private and, ultimately, embarrassing us in public. Thinking our silence, pride, and trill nature would always be a cloak to hide their misdeeds and selfish characters. Tuh!

Now, we are the dark that comes into light that they were warned about.

Rest easy knowing those who have wronged you will reap what they sow.

Be it through *God, Me (You), or Karma.*

Not So Fairy Tale

Writicide

Writing about us in past tense is killing me.

Will I be the first person to die by keystroke?

I'm bleeding across these pages—every word stabbing me

deeper as I attempt to journal my way into healing.

Unable to write it right seems like a fate worse than death.

Destined to eternally bleed and suffer as I constantly rewrite

our ending with no power to change the outcome.

TALE OF TWO FACES

Once upon a time I was a sweet girl

Too sweet

Too naive

Too trusting

Too understanding

Too loyal

Until situations showed I would continuously be devoured

by men in this world

So I became the eater instead

And it was a lonely place

Now trying to find a balance

I wade between two worlds

Living a double life

As the predator and the prey

Looking for the safehouse that will allow me to, once again,

confidently transform into that

Sweet

Trusting

Understanding

Loyal girl

The
Honeymoon

Genesis

We were two people trying to heal each other even though both our hearts were shattered

Somewhere between picking up the pieces and gluing our parts back together, we became inseparable

Fear Factor

From being scared to be with him to being afraid of living without him, I realized I'd found the love I never knew I needed. I stopped running from the inescapable, fell into his welcoming arms, and made myself right at home at the center of his heart.

Butterflies & Lies

He said, "I'll give you anything in this world. Just ask ..."

I replied, "You *are* my world. Can I have all of you?"

You In Danger, Girl!

GPS

He was infatuated with who he thought I was

Madly in love with the perception he'd created

I became imprisoned to his idealization

Drowned in the depths of his illusion

I was so engrossed in the alternate reality he envisioned

that I lost myself

And it's been hell trying to find my way back

Final Fantasy

It was my fantasy

Perfect guy

Perfect night

Wind blowing across my face

Water gently hitting the shore

Behind me was the presence of my black Adonis gazing at

the moonlight

Killer vibes

Sensuality in the air

This night had to be destined

Yearning overload

No escape

Under the stars commenced our first session

Heavy breathing

Fighting yet succumbing

Contact.Pause.Contact

Bombarded with reality

Enveloped in silence

Bodies fiending to go against logic and relapse

Atmosphere change

Same mood

Feelings too strong to fight

Piercing eyes

Soft kisses

From the couch to the floor

How could this be wrong?

It felt deliciously right

Oppositely horizontal

34.5 x 2

Wild actions of the starved and unnecessarily deprived

Bodies sweating

Unison movements

Worked our way to the end only we'd surmised

Reality hit

No expectations

The person from tonight will be a phantom by morning

Break away

Save face

Revel in the beauty

Refuse the inner mourning

Because

It was almost my fantasy

With the almost-perfect guy

On an almost-perfect night

Emotional Rollercoaster

Straightjacket

Insanity is

I can touch you

I can smell you

I can taste you

I can make love to you

But I cannot have you

One minute we are

The next we aren't

Other times we never were

Volatile goodbyes

Emotional reunions

Promises of trying

Riding the wave of hope

Crashing back into reality

Emotions running high

Then

Volatile goodbyes

Emotional reunions

Promises of trying

Insanity is

Message Sent, 3:22 AM

I feel like this has been our story: I'm always saying the wrong thing, and you don't say enough.

Then you say the wrong thing, and we switch places.

If I'm not mad at you, I'm sad and missing you, and you're oblivious.

Or I'm finding ways to just write the wrongs because it feels like the only place we'll ever be right is on paper.

Right …

I want things to be and feel right forever. Not only for a short-lived moment.

The Walking Dead

I smiled through the pain, but my eyes told a different tale

Still no one noticed the silent death taking pieces of me

Slowly chipping away at my core until I was a shell of the person I once was

Solely a warm body with a heart turned cold and a soul lost in the abyss of torment

Unable to find refuge or peace

Still radiating infectious healing energy to all except myself

Now that's superpower

Dying daily while simultaneously living

Situationship Woes

Circles

Disoriented circles

Dizzying cycles of repetition

Reciprocal romance morphed into unrequited love

Friends turned into strangers

That utterly nauseating ride

This go round was anything but merry

She escaped

Fighting to breathe again as it seemed her oxygen was left
with her tormentor

Revived by CPR from GOD and reacquainted with self-love

A rose arose from brokenness

Circles

Trick doors with no magical endings

No prince no charming

No white horse no valor

Cloaked in a bright smile that hid trauma and lack of
self-awareness

He couldn't save her or himself

Mazes

His feelings were an endless collection of paths leading to
dead ends

She entered his convoluted world where escapes were only
new beginnings for more of the same

Circles

Disoriented circles

My Disease

Why isn't there a rehab for love?

He's an addiction I can't seem to break no matter how hard

I try

One look

One visit

One inkling of another possible chance for us to work and

I'm right back overdosing on hope

Undevout

I need to constantly be reminded of GOD's love

so I can stop seeking it from men

incapable of giving it

TUG OF WAR

My body is a battlefield

North versus south in a war of wills

The north being the mind—strong and uncompromising

The south being the heart—soft and forgiving

Both ready to risk it all to be crowned sovereign over this

pending decision

I was told love was supposed to conquer all

but courtesy of his pride

I'm the one who took the fall

Depth after depth I plummeted while reaching out to grab a

piece of his heart

Hoping the softness of my touch

the soothing elements of my words

and affection in my eyes would lighten the dark

Darkness surrounded his emotions

like the black of midnight

Through tar and soot I fought my own inner death in an

attempt to save him

To save us

An unconquerable plight

Burned, scarred, and broken, I still forged ahead until the battle was no longer my own

As I lay in defeat I finally realized this was his conflict to duel alone

I waved the white flag and conceded then turned to walk away

My departure suddenly halted by the words I'd waited eons for him to proclaim

That moment was bittersweet

We were once again plagued by that devil called time

because even though my heart was loyally with him

no longer was my mind

I'd given every inch of me during that soul-wrenching crusade

I was emotionally bankrupt, and the roles had reversed

I was now the one needing to be saved

North or south

Which will reign triumphant

Do I feed the need or continue to fight the want

Because my body is a battlefield

That's Just That on That

I used to wear my loyalty like a badge of honor until I realized it was more of a curse than a gift

There was a time when loyalty was repaid with gratitude and reciprocal loyalty

Nowadays it gets you played

You'll just be playing yourself because my loyalty comes with a limit not a chain

The girl you love will quickly turn into a woman you don't even want to know

Almost Had It

Your feelings change quicker than your heart does

But when the heart turns cold

there's nothing left to be done

Stranger in my House

I'm no longer afraid to lose you

I'm more afraid of losing myself

Completely fearful of looking in the mirror one day and no

longer recognizing the person staring back at me

All in an effort of holding on to a person whom I never had

to begin with

CAPE

Sometimes the only way to save yourself

is to say goodbye

Denial

Straws

Was it really over, or were two ornery minds selfishly keeping two hearts from reconciling?

Or was wishful thinking postponing me from accepting the end we'd already inevitably reached?

Hansel & Gretel

And just like that the love finally died

The once flaming desire turned into hardened detachment

His inconsistencies led to a consistent trail of tears which

led her right out of his life

Happily Never After

Timing played a sick twisted joke on us

Had we met before the hurt or after the healing

our story would have been one fairytales are made of

Game Over

When dating or in relationships,

I always had uncertainties about my feelings.

Is this really love?

Am I good enough?

Is this genuine?

Am I doing too much or not enough?

But there was one feeling I was always unequivocally sure of …

The End

DRIFTERS

We said goodbye time after time

but the endings were just another intro to new beginnings

When we inevitability reached the end

it was without an announcement

without a profession

without a single word

Like a ship without a sail

we got lost and drifted apart slowly without direction

Betrayal

Message Sent, 9:38 PM

You should have left me alone while I was already healing from you. You selfishly chose to reopen that wound as if you were going to heal it with love, only to cut me even deeper. You knew what I wanted, required, deserved ... You promised you were ready to give it to me ... and I believed you. Because I was genuine, transparent, and forgiving (the very lesson God has been drilling into me), you're going to have to answer to Him for that.

THE LIONS' DEN

I tore myself apart continuously trying to fix him

Didn't even realize I was tearing off pieces of myself to build

him up

When I finally recognized what I'd done

I turned to ask for his help in mending the shattered pieces

of my overly trusting heart

only to shockingly watch him walk away—completely

whole—into the shell of another woman's arms

FAMILIAR STRANGERS

Heart racing, immobile, in utter disbelief

I saw him

The crowd parted as if this were fate planned in destiny

I wasn't prepared for that piercing familiar stare to look right

at me

The same pain in my heart was lodged in his eyes

He'd stolen our happiness, our future, devastating our lives

Disbelief, immobile, heart racing

I saw little him

His big brown eyes and innocent smile broke my soul

Memories of what was supposed to be in the days of old

Helplessness, walls closing, confronted with past demons

All eyes piercing through me

Words of strength from friends stopping my fleeing

Immobile, in utter disbelief, heart racing

I saw her

A carbon copy

of my

sloppy

seconds

Hating but within reason

Against me, they created treason

In utter disbelief, heart racing, immobile

I saw *them*

Suddenly, my view was unclear

Vision distorted by the onset of tears

Finally experiencing one of my worst fears

My dream and nightmare right in the flesh

Living it up

While I struggled daily

Feeling I had nothing left

That very moment sealed my eternity

Fuck love and whoever came with it

From then on, I'd only be about me

LEGALLY BLIND

My intuition has never failed me

But I've failed it numerous times

The hardest apology is always the one you have to issue

to yourself

Red's Rage

GOD. ME. OR KARMA (Redisms)

Let's be clear: When I want smoke, *I want all the smoke.* And I'm not stopping until Fire Marshall Bill or Smokey the Bear tells me to chill.

COLD WORLD

When I figured out it'd always be another *her*

I left because I knew it was only me

When he finally figured out there was only one *me*

it was too late because there had been one too many hers

Foolish

I think I'm over it

I swear I'm over you

But the vision of you with her causes me to relapse

It's funny how "just a friend" turned into "more than friends"

Silly me

Now I can't decipher whether I was a fool in love or simply

a fool

I Just Find It Funny ...

In a moment of weakness, I reached out and took an even deeper plunge from grace than the first time.

Message Sent, 2:17 AM

It was always you, not me.

And I was always too good for you, and you were never enough.

FALSE PROPHET

He wanted a project

I wanted a partner

It could never work

He claimed to be a healer

Taking pride in his calling to heal her

All while breaking me with lies soaked in selfishness

and saturated in deceit that he fed to me like scriptures

His ministry only showed up on what he thought would be

the hidden beaches of Cabo and forgotten Snapchat files

His bible class convened through text messages with the

different hers he was called to heal

His spiritual walk contained shortcuts that weren't biblical

but blessed him none the same with all his fleshly desires

A praised hypocrite

Hiding in plain sight under the guise of the falsely crucified

Used my respect for spirituality to move stealthily like a

snake in the garden

Cried to my face in the ninth hour not to be forsaken after

his transgressions were laid at my feet by someone other

than him

I offered my body and heart again like a sacrificial lamb

Only to watch him backslide into the same sin he'd denounced for a year

Drinking out of golden calves

Upset I didn't believe it was communion

All while I was praying my face off daily for us to be released from ~~forty~~ six years of wandering through his unsure desert

A revered Judas

Blasphemous behavior

Calling himself a man of God

A man? Of God?

More like a devil in disguise

A wolf in sheep's clothing

Backed by congregational blinders believing all claims are of false witness

But where there's numerous signs of smoke—there's a fire

"Hear O' Israel!"

There is only one God who is righteous, just, and, most of all, Omnipresent.

And *He* doesn't have respect for persons

So keep praying to the east because that mercy you wished upon my soul, you'll need tenfold

Bedtime Prayer

Now when I lay down to sleep

I pray the Lord my mind to keep

As it constantly loops and replays

Everything I allowed you to take

My trust, my hope, and my peace

But I know you'll pay for the hurt you've reaped

BIG MAD

Everything isn't fixed by habitual apologies

or coming-of-age excuses

But Karma has a way of collecting debts when you least

suspect

When she finally comes knocking at your door to collect all

the hearts you ran over on your journey to find yourself

I'll finally get closure

Forgive and Forget (FYM)

How do I forgive the person who destroyed my happy
ending?

The person I fault my demons and past hurts for—all for
nothing?

How can I forget when every small thing reminds me of him,
of us, reduced to simple memories?

All inescapable reminders of loss and deep regret for not
seeing what was right in front of me.

No, I can't forgive and forget.

More like fuck him as I leave to heal myself

and forget he ever existed.

Hindsight (Redisms)

If I knew I would be taking out this much trash in my adult years, I would have saved myself $50k in student loans and became a janitor.

STOLE

Why does the moon encourage melancholy?

The later it gets

the more my mind remembers

the harder my heart aches

Sleep becomes a clone of him

something else taken away from me

Regret is ...

giving the best of you to a person

who wasted your best years

only to leave you with the worst experience of what was

supposed to be the greatest feeling in the world

The Dark Knight

You falsely imprisoned my heart.

Now no one can get in to help me rescue it.

Who saves the saver?

Who heals the healer?

Who nurtures the nurturer?

For years, I rescued you.

Showed you how to break out of that box you were smothered in.

Now who is going to save me from you?

Not All Boyz
Turn in II Men

I wish I could cry, and every single fallen tear eradicates the resentment and anger I feel from the depths of my being. Then all these ill feelings and memories could evaporate as soon as my water ran dry.

Shell Shocked

I damaged myself wanting to see the best in you, when it seems your only goal was to see how much of your worst I could tolerate.

Suffering in silence only made me susceptible to more hurt.

Confronting your misdeeds resulted in being labeled crazy and overreacting.

Damned if I did, damned if I didn't.

A double-edged sword that left its imprint all over my mind.

Now those who truly attempt to show me their best are met with a person who only expects the worst.

THE WONDERING WANDERER

It hurt too good to really be love

That's how I knew it wasn't

Still I clung to the familiarity of pain

Like a baby with a blankie

Because this is what I knew ... the only thing I've known

It had always been my reality

Dysfunction dipped in lust

buried in hopes

draped in dreams of blossoming into true love

LOVE

Like an orphan I yearned the familiarity of a place

a heart I could call a home

My home

Instead I was doomed to be a wanderer

wondering

Always wondering what could have been

But knowing deep down if it were meant to be

we would have been

Déjà Vu

I was here before

The feelings were so familiar

Heart and mind playing tug of war

as my body awaited the winner

It's insane

because the culprit of my turmoil was never the same

They all mirrored each other in likeness

but had different names

But the hurt they left was collective

It continued to build as each one passed through

taking a piece of my innocence

no matter how hard I attempted to protect it

Still the tears won't fall

even as I sit and reminisce on how I risked it all ...

again and again

Only to end up in the same place

same situation

same feelings

with a different you

Praying for different results

but each time

it ends in déjà vu

OFF OF YOU

Never thought the pain would subside

Thought I was destined to die from a broken heart

A complete loss of pride

My failure personified

Gave all of me

Vulnerability

Even those parts I tried to hide

You begged to see

Said you needed to experience

all the makings of me

Then to up and leave

because I didn't measure up to your vision

The perfect image you'd constructed of who you thought I was

became my prison

My reality

Shackled

to your fantasy

Settled for scraps

Tearing myself apart

trying to find where I lacked

me being me

Wasn't good enough to choose

But the perfect choice

for you to use

to build yourself back up

better than ever

Using my heart

like a stepladder

Even I gotta admit

shit was clever

Let's hope you can maintain

this newfound strength

and sense of self that you claim

But if you can't

wouldn't that be a shame

'Cause you lost your pusher

Better yet

you pushed her

out of your life

to live a life

for them

Guess it never was

us vs. *them*

or me & you

It was always you

Only you

But you're now GOD or Karma's problem

I'm finally off of you

December Babies

Birthdays used to be for celebrating

Now they serve as a reminder of fake love

and real loss

and the only yearly interactions we're guaranteed

Rebound

Trading Places

The day I received confirmation of that ultimate betrayal was

the day we ironically crossed paths

Only out to fulfill a promise

I was fuming but hid it behind one of my many masks

DJ iLLa wrecking the ones and twos

The healing balm of Hennessy traveling down my throat

strong and smooth

Thoughts of the past

became a thing of the past

Finally living in the moment

for just a moment

When I connected with a pair of the most perfect intense

almond-shaped eyes

Over six feet tall fully bearded with skin reminiscent of

creamy peanut butter

baby boy was an entire vibe

Finessed my way into his space and found an excuse to rub

his beard

Engaged in a little cat-and-mouse banter while whispering

into each other's ear

He rewarded me with a smile showcasing a flawless set of teeth

Right then I knew I'd be staying in his presence for the remainder of the night

No other guy in the entire party could compete

Numbers exchanged

Plans to talk later arranged

One night

turned into every night

Like a teenage love affair

You go to sleep first no you go to sleep

Almond eyes was almost perfect

The timing wasn't fair

although the connection didn't care

No matter what I thought

I couldn't deny it was there

So was he

Always there

And when he wasn't

He wished he could be

Two jaded to believe

Judgment still too cloudy to conceive

He was the real deal

But I was still real scared

And real unhealed

Using sarcasm and distance as my shield

to push him away

Wasn't like he was going to stay

They never did anyway

Right?

He wasn't them

and they could never be him

Facts I knew

Didn't matter

I still withdrew

My time

My heart

ME

Killed the vibe

Went back to dance with the devil in disguise

Only to realize the devil was still a lie

Now I'm watching the real deal

who was always there

from a distance

Swear it ain't fair

He was worth the fight

But I realized too late

Now I was the issue

I'd turned into the men I hate

The realization hit like a ton of bricks

As I replayed my actions and my words

Stomach in knots knowing this time it was me who wasn't shit

It was vital I faded to black to mend those broken parts

Praying he'd be willing to rekindle what we had in the future

If no other woman had already stolen his heart

HOMESICK

He's not you.

But I don't want you anymore.

Or do I?

The constant battle of my past invading my present, making me miss what tried to destroy me.

Nostalgia totally obliterating the trail of hurt, only emphasizing those good feelings.

That euphoric purgatory holding me hostage as I internally battle whether to try one more time or let go.

My one wish is for confirmation that I'm walking away from something that would have never come into fruition and not walking away from the sole place I could have called home.

SDRAWKCAB

You didn't want them because you couldn't have him.

You push them away because he didn't stay.

If you could be good and stupid for lust, why can't you allow

yourself to be head over heels for love?

Quick to give yourself yet hold your heart hostage.

Silly girl—choose those who choose you.

Stop falling for the one who wants to possess you because

you're a challenge for his ego to conquer

or because he needs your energy to feel alive.

Give the one who truly desires your heart a chance.

PARIS

The studio of love is where we finally connected

My father's namesake

The one who'd been making his intentions clear

Still playing around in the lions' den

My vision was foggy

Loyal to the unloyal

Missed a possibly good thing

Herbal essence in the air

As "Boo'd Up" blared

we shared a moment

I knew he could be my someone new

Getting over one by getting under another

The pattern

But I'd learned my lesson

It was time for growth

Too much in common to ignore

A genuine heart I couldn't deny

Curiosity connected us

Unbridled honesty and similar senses of humor solidified
the bond

Undertones of wanting more still brewing under the surface

Always the chaser instead of the one being chased

My comfort zone was imploding

The person he deserved was still hidden under so many layers

I couldn't find her

Had he seen her?

With laser-like vision he saw through me with ease

Shook

Needing another level of protection to feel secure

Friendzoned

Unbothered and unmoved he remained

Respected my space and decision

Became a confidant

One of the few to hear when I was silent

Seen my defenses crumble under the weight of hurt

Suffered watching me wounded

Wiped my tears when the religion I worshipped failed

No judgement

Only concern

A caring spirit with the best of intentions

What I needed but didn't think I deserved

Self-worth tied to a situation with no value

Fumbled the bag

Chose known pain over the unknown

A closeted masochist

with soul ties to a sadist

Forever losing to a fate that felt beyond the grips of my control

Not wanting to drag anyone else into my perpetual hell

I chose to be alone

One more friend turning into an enemy in the name of lust

or love wasn't another risk I was willing to take

CHILDISH

We pass over the one with promising potential for the known

nuisance too many times

Fighting and struggling for love has become so common that

we question the sincerity when it comes easily

Yet welcome mediocrity and inconsistency with open arms

and hearts

Out here believing good is good enough like incredible is a

figment of imagination

Succumbing to below-basic standards to cum

Or show we have someone

even though that someone is out here for everybody

This is the new reality of dating

Love in our generation

It's a joke

A full circus

And to think

most of us grew up afraid of clowns

Now we fall madly in love with them

ANECDOTE

She hurt you

You hurt me

I hurt him

The relentless cycle continues

Instead

You forgive her

I help you heal

You don't destroy me

And I don't taint him

Let's practice

Less falling back and more falling into understanding

Love heals when we allow it

~~Non-Muthafuckin'~~ Ex-Factor

Funny thing about exes, they always try to come back. Funny thing about me, I stopped allowing them to.

I had to get out of the habit of allowing people to waste my time more than once.

Acceptance

He finally called, and his voice triggered a feeling emptier

than the loneliness I battled each night

He'd taught me how to live without him

And I lived

Message Sent, 7:18 PM

I refuse to regret giving you love and showing you there's more to life because you needed it. You're a walking testimony that, even with my flaws, I have the power to heal a heart with my love and patience and help others become better. The personal cost was high, and someone else is getting the reward, but God never fails me, *ever*. And that's why I know I'll be okay.

Self-Reflection & Lessons

On 4Nem'Grave

Vow to be more vocal about who you are

what you want

and what you require

We've become too complacent

letting our futures hang in the balance of others' uncertainties

forever playing it safe in hopes they'll eventually realize what

you have to offer

Run at the first sign of anyone who is unsure and makes

you feel as if you can't question where you stand in their life

Prime

Don't lose your value waiting years for a man to appraise your worth

While your sense of self is depreciating he'll be splurging with the one who never allowed him to discount her

Leave and don't look back

Wait patiently for the love that will treat you like you're priceless

Let him deal with women who are only going to bankrupt him

He'll count his losses once you're gone

DEAD WEIGHT

I told him I loved him

that he was my world

and that all I ever wanted was to be with him

Then I left him behind for good

Why

Because I knew my heart was finally ready to break free

Free

Ready to feel after being held captive for an eternity

My heart was ready to take me soaring past the moon

and he was still afraid of heights

Barbara N' Shirley

No matter the circumstances, I will never bask in destroying another woman's hope

nor feel empowered by obliterating her fantasy of a happily-ever-after ending that all women dream about.

We're all out here trying to get it right and prepare for Mr. Right but still getting wronged even after promises were made to right the wrongs.

But we still stand—unknowingly united, an army of resilient brave soldiers on the forefront, refusing to be defeated in the battle of hearts.

You don't go to war against a warrior who's seen what you've seen and lived what you've lived.

You can't resent a woman whose eyes and words hold the same misery you know stems from the inconsistent, conditional love of an immature, unsure guy.

You simply wish her the best and hope she comes out better than you ever did.

Then walk away finally understanding you were never the problem, and he is no longer *your* problem.

Veteran

You can't be ashamed of the people, situations, and circumstances that shaped you into who you are today
After all
what's a warrior without war wounds

Stay Strapped

Protect your time

Protect your energy

Protect your heart

People will waste your time

leave you depleted of positive energy

and completely disregard your heart

The worst part of it all is that you'll blame yourself

It's dangerous having a good heart in a world of unemotional

vultures that feed off of genuine energy

Be sure to guard your priceless essence as if your life

depends on it

TF

It's ironic how failed romance makes us question ourselves
rather than the person who failed us
We are way too hard on ourselves while giving others free
passes that they only use to take us for granted

Disobedience

You'll break your own heart holding on to people and situations GOD told you to let go of. Some of our pain is self-inflicted and could have been avoided with obedience.

Accountability

Settling out of impatience or lack of faith that better exists has caused more disappointment than single ever could.

We claim to accept things "out of love," when it's really out of settling, low self-esteem, fear of abandonment, and being alone. Owning the role you played and coming to terms with what you allowed helps you heal faster.

Truly believing what's coming is better than what's gone is essential to moving forward. Always remember—You only lose what was never yours to keep.

Pain

Pain has the ability to truly make us find ourselves.

Soul Searching

Wanting to be in love to running scared from love

The battle continued

I harmfully found solace in my solitude and independence

that somehow became the bricks that built a fort of protection

around my heart

Now, layer by layer, a master of patience must practice his

craft as I unload these bricks

helping along the way when the burden gets too heavy for

me to bear

SOS

Every drink

Every tattoo

Every burst of anger

Every act of silent treatment

Every smile and laugh that didn't reach her eyes

told a story no one seemed to be able to read

An open book with hidden meanings

Only an avid reader with a keen ability of deciphering cryptic

messages could hear her cry

RESET

I continuously have to remind myself it's okay to feel all emotions
not exclusively strength and anger

That I must own all the things I have experienced
because the pain
rejection
misunderstandings
and regrets are all mechanisms to help me reach my next level

I gave myself permission to cry
be heartbroken
and angry
Then I took the necessary steps to overcome that toxic space once and for all
because my full potential needed me more than my past

Needed Me

I learned the hard way that there is nothing strong about being silent while you struggle
Our generation wears being a savage like a badge of honor
Meanwhile, I'm trying to salvage my emotions in a time where not having them is the wave

Public Enemy #1

It hurt ... like hell.

The truth isn't always an easy pill to swallow, but this one was indigestible.

Knowing I would eventually have to look the conspirator of my turmoil in the eye and acknowledge that they let me down was a blow that had me reeling for years.

Mixing light and dark to dull the ache until I felt nothing.

Party hopping to procrastinate that inevitable confrontation.

Trading quick lit nights for those long nights of insomnia.

Reality took my turn up and turned it all the way down until I had no choice but to confront my past.

With shaky hands and tears in my eyes, I picked up my phone to finally accost the person who had wronged me.

I opened the camera and confronted my reflection.

Accomplice

I handed him the weapon to murder me

Even came back for more of the same with each of my nine

lives until we killed all the love and light left in me

A co-conspirator to my own demise

No charges, but I was guilty

Sentenced to a life of mental prison

Replaying the many opportunities I'd had to stop my own

homicide

Retrospection

My biggest mistake was never turning my back for good

Letting love for him trump love for self

Blinded by what I wanted

Overlooked the true colors I was shown

Praised averageness

Made excuses for indifference

Enamored by the slightest effort

Destroyed because it was fleeting

Tied my esteem to his opinion like his name was Self

Based my happiness on his treatment

Forgot I, too, was a prize before I met him

and would still be when he was gone

Those things had nothing to do with him

and everything to do with me

While I can't honor disloyalty and outright manipulation

I can't get mad at someone for choosing to do what makes
them happy

I can't be upset if they believe they chose LOVE

All I can do is wish I had done the same sooner

TOUGH LOVE

It's not always *them*

Sometimes it's *you*

You have to realize your own toxicity

Until you heal yourself

find solace in your own space before poisoning someone

who only wants the best for you

Sink or Swim

Past trauma and consequences from bad decisions have a way of subconsciously plaguing our present.

At worst, they even destroy positive relationships and reinforce toxic ones.

It's imperative to really sit back and rectify the turmoil within to calm the storms that present as trust issues, cynicism, and anger.

My life jacket of comfortability had to be ripped away, causing me to drown in my own troubled waters before I unloaded unnecessary baggage from my sinking boat.

But in sink or swim times, I'll always survive.

To Thine Own Self Be True

Take time to learn, accept, and appreciate who you are at your core—just you.

Learn who you are as a person, not a label. You're so much more than that.

Accept your flaws and where you aren't perfect. Own who you are, and no one will ever be able to tell you otherwise nor take it from you.

Appreciate everything: the good, the bad, and all the chaos in between. It's how you learn and grow and how you take back your power.

Only when you truly love yourself unconditionally can you be able to see real love, welcome it and reciprocate it.

You will also see what isn't love and dismiss it before it latches on to you.

UNBREAKABLE

Time ... It either heals the wound or completely breaks the wounded.

Forgiveness

Conqueror

The pain taught me strength

The hurt birthed my resilience

Situations meant to tear me down only built me up stronger

Now I stand powerful, wearing my scars like badges of honor

Those scars, constant reminders that I looked the devil in

his eyes and won

FANETO

The moment I forgave him, I freed myself

I learned some stories are only meant to be chapters, not an entire book

These pages will forever hold the memories I have to release in order to move on

Growth

I could never hate the person who was a huge part of my growth, an instrumental force behind the person I am today
The person who knows my deepest secrets, regrets, and fears
It didn't work out, but not everything in life does
Separation doesn't always mean conflict—sometimes it just means growth

HEALING

I forgive because I know what it's like to need forgiveness from transgressions that occurred when I didn't love myself. Life and love aren't easy by any means, and we're all trying to navigate our way through it. People we meet are simply in different stages than we are at times. Forgive and pray for their healing as if it's your own. Even if you have to do it from a distance.

Rebirth

Humbled

One day, the person who broke you will be forced to admire your wholeness.

GLOW UP

I wanted to grow with you

Instead, I was forced to change on you

You will feel my growth and happiness from afar

The memories of my energy and love will haunt you until the day you leave this earth

You'll catch glimpses of my innocence in your future daughters and pray they won't be affected by the karma you have coming for stealing mine

Soon, you'll be left telling all who will listen, "I used to know her" as you watch me successfully conquer all those dreams I shared with you

Tragic

Albuterol (Redisms)

You can beg a man until you're blue in the face to act right
and choose you, but if you ain't the one, you ain't the one.

I got asthma, a full-time job, and a side hustle ...
I ain't got the time or breath for that anymore.
I don't know what I was thinking anyway.

No Future (Redisms)

You've now read through some of the situationships and life lessons that made me the person I am today.

You've seen my fears, my pain, my stupidity, and, ultimately (I hope), my growth.
If you've found yourself experiencing any of the situations you've read inside this book, repeat after me:

> My heart is not an orphanage
>
> My mission on this earth is not to nurture humans I didn't birth with love until they find their forever homes in someone else's heart
>
> My love isn't a 501(c)(3)
>
> Nor is the time I offer volunteer work—either we're working on *us*, or I'm going to be unemployed
>
> My name isn't Energizer
>
> I will no longer let people deplete me of my energy and toss me aside for a new set
>
> My self-worth and happiness start and end with *me*

I am *enough*

If they can't see it, then they're blind and
stupid

And I don't need to be with anyone who
needs to pick a struggle

I learned my lessons the hard way; hopefully, you don't have
to. Please hear me loud and clear—like Angela in *Why Did
I Get Married* loud: From this moment forth, if a person isn't
ready for what you're ready for, if they're saying they're
unsure, or they need more time, or are too busy, etc., *let.
them.go.* They belong to the streets.

Thank you all for coming to my TED Talk.

Sincerely,

Tina Red - The Wordsmith

Thank you for reading *God, Me, Or Karma*

If you enjoyed this book, please leave an online review.

KEEP UP WITH TINA RED

Email: info@tinaredthewordsmith.com

Website: www.tinaredthewordsmith.com

Instagram: @tina_red_wordsmith

Facebook: https://www.facebook.com/tinaredthewordsmith/

Twitter: @tinaredwordsmth

Made in the USA
Columbia, SC
19 February 2020